A Note to Parents and Teachers

Kids can imagine, kids can laugh and kids can learn to read with this exciting new series of first readers. Each book in the Kids Can Read series has been especially written, illustrated and designed for beginning readers. Humorous, easy-to-read stories, appealing characters and topics, and engaging illustrations make for books that kids will want to read over and over again.

To make selecting a book easy for kids, parents and teachers, the Kids Can Read series offers three levels based on different reading abilities:

Level 1: Kids Can Start to Read

Short stories, simple sentences, easy vocabulary, lots of repetition and visual clues for kids just beginning to read.

Level 2: Kids Can Read with Help

Longer stories, varied sentences, increased vocabulary, some repetition and visual clues for kids who have some reading skills, but may need a little help.

Level 3: Kids Can Read Alone

More challenging topics, more complex sentences, advanced vocabulary, language play, minimal repetition and visual clues for kids who are reading by themselves.

With the Kids Can Read series, kids can enter a new and exciting world of reading!

Alexander Graham Bell

For Pierson Matthew White and all of the
telephone calls he'll make in his life — E.M.

For my family — A.K.

The publisher and author wish to express their gratitude and appreciation to
Brian Wood, Curator, Bell Homestead National Historic Site, for his review of the
text and art. While every effort has been made to ensure accuracy, any errors are
the responsibility of the author and publisher.

Kids Can Press acknowledges the financial support of the Government of
Ontario, through the Ontario Media Development Corporation's Ontario Book
Initiative; the Ontario Arts Council; the Canada Council for the Arts; and the
Government of Canada, through the BPIDP, for our publishing activity.

Published in Canada by	Published in the U.S. by
Kids Can Press Ltd.	Kids Can Press Ltd.
29 Birch Avenue	2250 Military Road
Toronto, ON M4V 1E2	Tonawanda, NY 14150

www.kidscanpress.com

Edited by Jennifer Stokes and David MacDonald
Designed by Marie Bartholomew
Printed and bound in Singapore

Educational consultant: Maureen Skinner Weiner, United Synagogue Day School,
Willowdale, Ontario.

The hardcover edition of this book is smyth sewn casebound.
The paperback edition of this book is limp sewn with a drawn-on cover.

CM 07 0 9 8 7 6 5 4 3 2 1
CM PA 07 0 9 8 7 6 5 4 3 2 1

Library and Archives Canada Cataloguing in Publication

MacLeod, Elizabeth
    Alexander Graham Bell / written by Elizabeth MacLeod;
illustrated by Andrej Krystoforski.

ISBN 978-1-55453-001-4 (bound) ISBN 978-1-55453-002-1 (pbk.)

1. Bell, Alexander Graham, 1847–1922 — Juvenile literature.
2. Inventors — Canada — Biography — Juvenile literature. 3. Inventors —
United States — Biography — Juvenile literature. I. Krystoforski, Andrej, 1943–
II. Title.

TK6143.B4M32 2007   j621.385092   C2006-903284-X

Kids Can Press is a **ʃᴏᴦᴜs**™ Entertainment company

Alexander Graham Bell

Written *by* Elizabeth MacLeod
Illustrated by Andrej Krystoforski

Kids Can Press

Next time you pick up the phone to call a friend, say thanks to Alexander Graham Bell. He invented the telephone more than 130 years ago.

Alexander's invention changed the world! It helps you keep in touch with family and friends. You can order things you need over the telephone. If someone is hurt, you can phone for help.

Alexander — who was called Aleck by his family — was born in 1847 in Scotland. He and his brothers, Melville and Edward, had fun playing and building things. They once invented a talking doll that sounded so real it fooled a neighbor!

Aleck

It's no wonder that Aleck was interested in sound and inventing. His mother could not hear well. And Aleck's father was a speech teacher. He helped people learn to speak clearly. Aleck's dad even invented a way to help deaf people learn to speak.

When Aleck was 21, he became a speech teacher, just like his father. Aleck taught many deaf children how to speak.

It is difficult for deaf children to learn how to talk. They cannot learn words by hearing other people say them. And they cannot hear if they are saying words correctly.

Aleck invented different ways to teach his students. For instance, the children would put their fingers on Aleck's throat while he said a word. The children could feel how their throats should move when they said that word.

By the time Aleck was 23, both of his brothers had died from a disease that makes breathing very difficult. Then Aleck got the same sickness.

Aleck's parents decided to take him somewhere with clean air. They hoped this would save his life. In 1870, the Bells moved to Brantford, Ontario, in Canada.

Here, Aleck spent most of his time resting. But he also did experiments to learn more about sound. For hours, Aleck sang into his piano. When he did, the wire strings inside the piano made sounds. Aleck wondered why.

Before long, Aleck felt healthy again. He got a job at a school for deaf children in the United States. Soon he was on his way to Boston, Massachusetts.

Aleck was happy to go because he liked teaching. And he knew there were many scientists in Boston. He wanted to talk to them about his experiments with sound.

In Boston, Aleck began teaching at the school. Sometimes he used feathers to help students see if they were making sounds correctly.

Aleck also taught students at his home, after school. This gave him extra money to do more experiments with sound.

At night, Aleck often stayed up late doing his sound experiments.

Aleck was trying to find a way to send the human voice through wires. That would let people who are far apart talk to each other.

Aleck knew he had to hurry. Many other scientists were trying to figure out how to send speech through wires. Aleck wanted to be first!

Aleck hired a man named Thomas Watson to help him. The two men experimented almost every night. They were close to sending the human voice through wires!

On March 10, 1876, Aleck was in one room. He had a mouthpiece connected by wire to another room. There, Thomas had equipment to receive the words Aleck spoke into the mouthpiece.

"Mr. Watson — Come here — I want to see you," said Aleck.

Thomas raced in. He had heard Aleck's words. They had traveled through the wire. Aleck had sent the first telephone message!

Later that summer, Aleck visited his
parents in Brantford. On August 3, he set
up his invention in the nearby town of
Mount Pleasant. That night, people there
listened to people in Brantford, which was
8 km (5 mi.) away. Everyone was amazed.

On August 10, people gathered in Paris, Ontario, to see Aleck's incredible invention. Soon they heard the voices of people in Brantford, which was 13 km (8 mi.) away. Aleck's telephone was a success!

At first, some people did not like the telephone. It was new and they did not understand it. They wondered if it could spread germs. Others worried that the telephone could hear everything they said, even if they were not on the phone!

Aleck put on shows to help people get used to his invention.

Aleck kept working with the telephone. And he had fallen in love — with Mabel Hubbard, a young woman who was one of his students.

Mabel was deaf, but she had learned how to watch people's lips to see what they were saying. When Aleck and Mabel went walking at night, they spent most of their time standing under streetlights. Mabel needed the light to see Aleck's lips when he talked. If the couple went on a buggy ride, Mabel brought a candle.

Aleck and Mabel were soon married.
They had two daughters, Elsie and Marion.

In 1885, Aleck and his family began spending summers on Cape Breton Island in Nova Scotia, Canada. He built a large home there. It was so big that it had eleven fireplaces! Aleck built a lab, too, so he could have a place to do more inventing.

Aleck loved relaxing at his summer home. He liked to float in a nearby lake for hours, just thinking.

Aleck kept inventing. He created a machine to test how well people could hear. He also invented an air conditioner, an iceberg finder and more. Aleck even built airplanes.

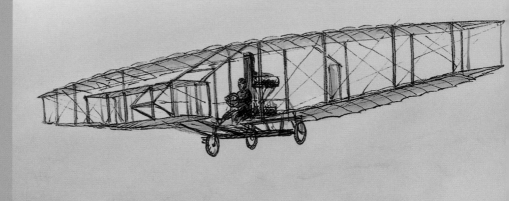

By now Aleck was well known because of his inventions. Sometimes he got tired of his most famous one, the telephone. Aleck often wrapped a towel around his telephone so he would not hear it ring. "Now a man can think!" he would say.

In 1915, Aleck made the first telephone call that went all the way across North America. From New York, New York, he called his friend Thomas Watson in San Francisco, California.

"Mr. Watson — Come here — I want to see you!" said Aleck. Thomas said he would be happy to come. But it would take much longer this time!

San Francisco

New York

Aleck died in 1922. During his funeral, telephone companies across North America turned off all phones. This was to show that people would never forget Aleck and his telephone—an invention that changed the world.

More facts about Aleck

• Aleck was born on March 3, 1847. He died on August 2, 1922.

• When Aleck answered the phone he said, "Hoy! Hoy!" instead of "Hello!"

• Aleck was a good friend of Helen Keller. She was a famous writer and public speaker who was deaf and blind.

• You can visit the house where Aleck lived in Brantford. You can also tour the Alexander Graham Bell National Historic Site. It's on Cape Breton Island near Aleck's home there.